Original title:
Stars in My Sleep

Copyright © 2024 Creative Arts Management OÜ
All rights reserved.

Author: Adeline Fairfax
ISBN HARDBACK: 978-9916-90-740-5
ISBN PAPERBACK: 978-9916-90-741-2

Dreaming Upward in Starlit Genesis

In the cradle of night, whispers play,
Awakening dreams that drift and sway.
Silken threads of hope entwine,
Weaving futures in a starlit line.

Beneath the cosmos, hearts take flight,
Chasing shadows, embracing light.
With every pulse, a story we draw,
In the stillness, we feel the awe.

A Symphony of Night's Luminous Whispers

The moon hums softly in the deep,
As stars converse in secrets they keep.
Notes of twilight glide through the air,
Echoes of magic, rich and rare.

Each flicker, a tale of longing told,
A symphony of dreams, brave and bold.
Together they dance, a gentle refrain,
Binding the heart with invisible chain.

Canvas of Dark, Dotted with Light

Black velvet stretching, wide and vast,
A canvas where dreams are cast.
Dotted with pinpricks of radiance bright,
Illuminating the silence of night.

Colors swirl in the depths unknown,
In each spark, a universe grown.
Gazing upward, we find our way,
Living for the magic of the sway.

The Light That Cradles the Night

Stars flicker softly in the dark,
Guiding dreams with their gentle spark.
The moon's embrace, a silvery glow,
Whispers secrets that only night can know.

In shadows deep, where silence reigns,
Laughter from the past still remains.
Each twinkle tells of stories old,
In the heart of night, mysteries unfold.

Dreaming of Cosmic Wonders

In the vastness of the sky so wide,
Adventures await on a stellar ride.
Planets dance with a vibrant grace,
Inviting souls to embrace their space.

Comets streak with a fiery tail,
Whispers of magic in the cosmic veil.
Galaxies spin in a grand ballet,
Where dreams of stardust drift away.

The Echo of Heavenly Whispers

Softly spoken from realms above,
Messages wrapped in celestial love.
Voices rise like a lilting breeze,
Carried through the night with effortless ease.

They sing of hope and distant lands,
Where hearts unite and time expands.
In every echo, a secret shared,
Binding the dreams of those who dared.

Serenity Among the Celestial Bodies

In tranquil depths of the cosmic sea,
Where stars align in harmony.
Gentle orbits in a dance divine,
Whispers of peace in the astral design.

The quiet hum of the universe sings,
Creating solace in the night it brings.
Among the bodies, a calm resides,
In the heart of space, true beauty hides.

A Tapestry Woven in Dreamlight

In twilight's arms, the shadows play,
Threads of silver dance and sway.
Whispers of night in soft embrace,
Dreams unfold in timeless space.

Stars like jewels in velvet skies,
Map the paths where magic lies.
Each heartbeat sings a secret tune,
Awakening the sleeping moon.

Celestial Dreams in a Whispered Tone

Softly glows the evening star,
Drawing dreams from lands afar.
In the hush of night's caress,
Yearning hearts find sweet success.

Melodies of vast expanse,
Lure the soul to dream and dance.
With each breath, the cosmos sighs,
Whispered wonders fill the skies.

Night's Harmonious Glow

Amid the dark, a gentle light,
Icons of the tranquil night.
Harmony in whispered breeze,
Cradled softly among the trees.

Moonlit paths weave tales sublime,
Echoes of the quiet time.
In every shadow, secrets dwell,
Crafting stories we can't tell.

Enchanted by the Celestial Night

Underneath the starry dome,
Wanderers find their hearts at home.
Galaxies in midnight's grasp,
Futures twinkling in their clasp.

Each comet's tail, a fleeting kiss,
Promises in the cosmic bliss.
Underneath this vast expanse,
Life is but a twinkling dance.

Radiant Veils of Night's Embrace

Beneath the stars, the shadows play,
Whispers of dreams drift far away.
Moonlit rivers softly flow,
In night's embrace, our hopes aglow.

Veils of silence wrap the world,
As the cosmic dance is unfurled.
Each twinkle tells a tale so bright,
In the hush of soft twilight.

Crickets sing their evening song,
While fireflies flicker all night long.
A tranquil heart finds peace to keep,
In the depths where starlight seep.

Awake, we linger, lost in awe,
As night's inventions gently draw.
With radiant veils, time stands still,
In the magic that dreams instill.

Galactic Dreams and Hidden Paths

In the expanse where secrets lie,
Galaxies spin in the velvet sky.
Dreams arise on cosmic winds,
As the universe begins and ends.

Stars ignite like sparks of hope,
Guiding souls to gracefully cope.
Hidden paths beneath the night,
Whispers of fate in pure delight.

Celestial highways weave and bend,
Where thought and time seamlessly blend.
Each heartbeat echoes in the vast,
Reminding us of connections cast.

Journey forth through cosmic seas,
With every wish carried by breeze.
Galactic dreams await our tread,
On hidden paths where angels led.

When the Cosmos Calls

When the cosmos calls, we must reply,
With the spark of wonder deep in our eye.
Echoes of stardust whisper near,
Summoning hearts to conquer fear.

Voices of nebulae softly sing,
In the night, our spirits take wing.
Celestial forces play their tune,
Harmonized under the watchful moon.

Hearts entwined in the cosmic glow,
Journeying where the wild winds blow.
Infinity beckons with open arms,
Drawing us near with its ancient charms.

Let the heavens guide each beat,
Where the universe and dreams meet.
When the cosmos calls with its embrace,
We rise together, lost in grace.

Between the Galaxies of Thought

Between the galaxies of thought we roam,
Seeking knowledge, finding home.
Ideas flourish in the starry expanse,
As minds ignite in stellar dance.

Fragments of wisdom drift and weave,
Exploring realms we can't perceive.
Each notion shines with radiant light,
Illuminating the depths of night.

Curiosity fuels our endless flight,
Through the cosmos, we chase the light.
Connections form like constellations bright,
In the tapestry of insight's height.

Together we journey, hand in hand,
Searching for truths in a boundless land.
Between the galaxies, our dreams align,
In the universe where our thoughts entwine.

Dreamscapes of Astral Light

In the hush of the twilight glow,
Stars whisper secrets, tales untold.
Moonbeams dance on the silver snow,
Woven dreams in the night unfold.

Floating softly on cosmic streams,
We drift through realms of endless night.
In the heart of our tender dreams,
We find our path in the astral light.

With every shimmer, our spirits soar,
Galaxies call in a gentle sigh.
In this vastness, we seek for more,
A tapestry stitched by the sky.

Awake in the magic, we may find,
The echoes of love that intertwine.
Through these dreamscapes, our souls aligned,
We'll wander the stars where the heart shines.

Lullabies of the Night Sky

Close your eyes to this gentle night,
The moon croons softly, pure delight.
Stars hum a tune, peaceful and bright,
Lullabies whisper, hearts take flight.

Clouds like pillows drift slowly by,
Carrying dreams on their feathery wings.
In this stillness, let out a sigh,
As night unveils the joy it brings.

Crickets play in the meadow fair,
Their music drifts through the dusky air.
Each note a promise, soft and rare,
Wrapped in moonlight, free from care.

As slumber calls you, heed its song,
Let the night cradle you with ease.
In its embrace, you will belong,
Until dawn kisses the world with peace.

When Galaxies Embrace My Dreams

Floating softly in twilight's breath,
Galaxies bloom with colors bright.
In dreams, they dance, defying death,
    Embracing me in starry light.

Each star a story of love and grace,
    Whispers of hope in a cosmic sea.
In their embrace, I find my place,
Where endless wonders set me free.

Wander through constellations wide,
Holding the dreams that never fade.
In their warmth, I take my stride,
    A celestial journey, unafraid.

When morning breaks, I'll hold them tight,
These visions spun in the night's embrace.
For even as dawn steals the light,
I carry their magic, time can't erase.

Cosmic Serenade in the Quiet Hours

Under a vault of endless skies,
Soft echoes murmur through the dark.
In the silence, the universe sighs,
A cosmic serenade ignites a spark.

Stars twinkle like jewels afar,
Each one a note in the night's refrain.
We wander through realms where dreams are,
Woven with stardust, free of pain.

In the stillness, our hearts align,
Chasing the whispers of the night breeze.
With every heartbeat, we intertwine,
Lost in the magic, souls at ease.

As twilight fades and dawn draws near,
These melodies linger, soft and clear.
With every moment, we hold most dear,
The cosmic serenade, forever here.

Night's Gentle Embrace

In shadows deep where whispers grow,
The stars above begin to glow.
A tranquil hush enfolds the night,
As dreams take wing in silver light.

Beneath the veil of twinkling skies,
The moonlight soft, a sweet disguise.
In quiet corners hearts align,
In Night's embrace, all souls entwine.

The world asleep, time stands still,
A symphony of night, a gentle thrill.
With every breath, the peace we find,
In this cocoon, our hearts unbind.

So let us wander hand in hand,
Through wonders wrought by night's command.
Where every sigh and starry glance,
Invites us to a sacred dance.

The Cosmic Cradle

In cosmic arms where stardust sways,
The universe sings in dazzling rays.
Galaxies whirl in waltzing grace,
A timeless dance in endless space.

Nebulae bloom in colors bright,
A canvas painted with pure light.
We drift on whispers of the breeze,
In this vast cradle, hearts find ease.

The planets hum their ancient tune,
Underneath the glowing moon.
Each twinkling star, a dreamer's call,
In the cradle's hold, we rise and fall.

So take my hand, let's journey far,
Through stellar fields where wishes are.
In the cosmic weave, let spirits soar,
Together bound forevermore.

Wandering Through Cosmic Haze

Amidst the stars, in twilight's gaze,
We find ourselves in cosmic haze.
With every step, a new frontier,
A universe that draws us near.

The Milky Way, a velvet trail,
Where whispers of the ancients prevail.
In shades of blue and softest grey,
Our hearts ignite in grand ballet.

Galactic winds whisper and play,
As we meander, lose our way.
Through twists of time, we shall explore,
The mysteries that space has in store.

So let us drift on dreams sublime,
In this vast realm, we dance with time.
With every breath, we weave our fate,
Wandering through the cosmic state.

Ethereal Dreams of Infinite Hues

In twilight realms where colors blend,
Ethereal dreams, our souls transcend.
Each shade a whisper, soft and rare,
In the canvas of the midnight air.

With every heartbeat, visions bloom,
In spaces filled with fragrant gloom.
A tapestry of night's embrace,
Where time itself finds solace, grace.

The echoes of our laughter ring,
In unity, our spirits sing.
With every star that lights the night,
We chase the dreams, embrace the light.

So close your eyes and let them flow,
These ethereal dreams that softly glow.
In hues of wonder, let us play,
As dawn awaits to greet the day.

Lunar Secrets Unfold

In the hush of night's embrace,
Moonlight dances, soft and pale.
Whispers echo in the space,
Tales of dreams and secrets sail.

Silver beams on tranquil seas,
Casting shadows on the shore.
Every ripple, every breeze,
Holds the stories of yore.

Stars awaken with a sigh,
Illuminating paths untold.
As I gaze at the sky,
Lunar secrets slowly unfold.

Underneath this starlit dome,
Hearts are tethered, souls aligned.
In this vast celestial home,
Hidden truths are redefined.

Astral Reveries

Floating through the midnight air,
Stars like diamonds in a cloak.
Dreams drift softly without care,
In this realm where spirits soak.

Winds of time begin to weave,
Threads of light, a cosmic tale.
In each moment, we believe,
Astral visions cannot fail.

Gentle whispers through the night,
Calling souls to join the dance.
In the glow of silver light,
Every heartbeat finds its chance.

As I close my weary eyes,
The universe begins to sway.
Lost in deep, celestial sighs,
I dream the night softly away.

Midnight's Guiding Lights

The clock strikes twelve, all is still,
Stars ignite the velvet sky.
Guiding lights on every hill,
Whispers of the night's soft sigh.

Through the dark, a path is shown,
Every glimmer, every glow.
In the stillness, seeds are sown,
For the dreams we dare to grow.

Moonlit shadows softly dance,
Echoing the heart's delight.
In their rhythm, find your chance,
Midnight brings the world to light.

With each beat, the cosmos breathes,
Infinite stories yet to weave.
In this night, the heart believes,
Midnight's secrets we receive.

The Sky Within My Eyes

Gaze into the depths of night,
Count the stars that shine so bright.
In their glow, I see the fire,
Of the dreams that lift me higher.

Clouds like whispers drift on by,
Carrying the echoes high.
Every breath, a blend of grace,
In the vast and boundless space.

Colors swirl in twilight's blush,
Painting feelings in a hush.
In this moment, worlds collide,
The sky within, my heart's guide.

Every glance, a universe,
In the darkness, I immerse.
Holding close what dreams comprise,
Finding peace within my eyes.

The Silver Threads of Dreams

In the twilight, whispers roam,
Silver threads weave a soft dome.
Glimmers of hopes, shining bright,
Tangled in the fabric of night.

Stars wink from the heavens above,
Guiding hearts wrapped in love.
Each thread a story, a gentle kiss,
Crafted in shadows, a world of bliss.

The breeze carries tales untold,
In silver whispers, secrets unfold.
Woven in silence, dreams take flight,
In the arms of the moonlit night.

Rest now, weary soul, and see,
The silver threads hold your key.
To worlds where wishes come alive,
In dreams, our spirits truly thrive.

Chasing Comets in Slumber

As I drift in soft embrace,
Chasing comets through endless space.
Dreams sparkle with cosmic light,
Trails of wonder in the night.

Through nebulas, I glide and soar,
Captured by the universe's lore.
In the silence, stars collide,
On wings of night, my hopes abide.

Each comet's tail, a fleeting glance,
Inviting heart and soul to dance.
With every wish upon a spark,
I find my place within the dark.

So let me dream, let me fly,
Chasing comets across the sky.
In the realms where stardust glows,
I craft a world that only I know.

The Universe's Silent Voice

In the stillness of a cosmic night,
Whispers of the universe take flight.
In every star, a story we hear,
The silent voice that draws us near.

Galaxies swirl in a dance divine,
Echoes of time through space intertwine.
With every glance, a truth unveiled,
In the depths of silence, souls are hailed.

From distant worlds, the murmurs call,
Encircling dreams that rise and fall.
The universe speaks in a tender tone,
A symphony for the heart, all alone.

So listen closely, feel the grace,
The silent voice we all embrace.
In unity, we find our place,
Connected by the cosmic trace.

Luminous Thoughts in the Dark

In the quiet shadows where shadows creep,
Luminous thoughts awaken from sleep.
Gentle glows of clarity arise,
Illuminating corners, cutting ties.

In the whispering night, ideas bloom,
Casting aside the lingering gloom.
Each notion glistens like a star,
Guiding us gently, near and far.

As thoughts meander through twilight's grace,
They find their way, a hidden space.
In the dark, creativity thrives,
A dance of brilliance, where hope survives.

Embrace the silence, let it spark,
Luminous thoughts ignite the dark.
In the heart of night, freedom unfolds,
Stories of wisdom, waiting to be told.

The Nebula of Night

In the heart of the dark sky,
Stars whisper soft and low.
Nebulae twirl and sigh,
In colors that gently glow.

Mysteries swirl and dance,
A cosmic ballet unfurled.
Each speck a fleeting chance,
In the vastness of the world.

Dreamers gaze, eyes alight,
Tracing patterns unknown.
The nebula wraps tight,
In a silence like a tone.

A canvas of endless space,
Painting wonders above.
In the night's warm embrace,
Cosmic wonders we love.

Cosmic Embrace in Slumber

Silently the stars twinkle,
In shadows of eternal night.
Dreams drift and hearts crinkle,
Wrapped in soft starlight.

Galaxies spin and weave,
In a cosmic cradle deep.
Whispers of time believe,
As the universe falls asleep.

Gentle comets glide through,
A dance of light and grace.
In this realms' loving hue,
Every soul finds its place.

In slumber's sweet embrace,
Time hangs like a thread.
All fears now efface,
In the depths of dreams spread.

When Light Meets Darkness

A flicker in the still,
Where shadows curl and sway.
Light bends to fill the chill,
As night transforms to day.

A dance of dark and bright,
In harmony they play.
Moments of pure delight,
In the dawn's gentle ray.

Stars bid their soft goodbye,
As the sky blushes wide.
Darkness whispers a sigh,
With the dawning tide.

When light meets the dark,
A promise in the skies.
A canvas, a spark,
Where new life always lies.

Echoes of Celestial Echoes

In the void, echoes call,
Whispers of ages past.
Stars that rise and fall,
Craft stories unsurpassed.

Each twinkle speaks a tale,
Of worlds beyond our might.
In silence, dreams prevail,
Echoes of pure delight.

Galaxies serenade,
In the vastness of time.
Cosmic memories fade,
In rhythms so sublime.

From darkness to the dawn,
Echoes softly glide.
In the night's gentle yawn,
Celestial truths abide.

Night's Tapestry of Glimmering Wishes

In twilight's grasp, soft lights appear,
Gentle whispers beckon near.
Each star a hope, a dream to hold,
In night's embrace, our tales unfold.

Beneath the dark, where shadows play,
We cast our hopes, let wishes sway.
Each twinkle shines, a silent prayer,
In the night's canvas, we lay bare.

Glistening threads in azure skies,
Woven wishes as time flies.
We sail through dreams, on cosmic streams,
Where night's enchantment paints our themes.

With every breath, the heavens sigh,
As moonbeams dance, we drift on high.
In this vast space, our hearts are free,
In night's tapestry, it's you and me.

Celestial Dreams and Moonlit Murmurs

Lost in dreams of silver light,
Where whispers flow through velvet night.
The moon smiles down, a guiding friend,
On these soft murmurs, our hearts depend.

Stars draw lines in endless dance,
Inviting us to take a chance.
With every spark, a story spins,
In celestial realms, where hope begins.

Beneath this dome, we drift and sway,
Chasing wishes that softly play.
The night unfolds its mystic schemes,
In the magic of celestial dreams.

Each sigh and shimmer, a breath of peace,
In moonlit glades, our worries cease.
Together we weave, under endless streams,
In the harmony of our moonlit dreams.

Wandering Through Nebulae of Thought

In realms where colors swirl and blend,
Thoughts drift like stars, they bend and wend.
Messages lost in cosmic haze,
In nebulous clouds, our minds ablaze.

Through endless paths of swirling light,
We seek the truth in shadows bright.
Each journey whispers secrets deep,
In the void, where thoughts do leap.

Eclipsed reflections in starlit seas,
Awaken dreams with every breeze.
We wander far, through cosmic sighs,
In nebulae where silence lies.

With every step, we weave our fate,
In the vastness, we'll celebrate.
Together we thread through this night's cloth,
Unraveling thoughts, our minds betroth.

Echoes of Starlit Fantasies

In echoes soft of starlit nights,
Whispers of dreams float to new heights.
Each twinkle tells a tale so grand,
Of wishes captured in heartfelt sand.

Through night's embrace, our spirits roam,
In fantasies woven, we find home.
With every star, a map unfolds,
In echoes where our story holds.

The rhythm glows in tender beams,
With every pulse, a dance of dreams.
We trace our path through cosmic streams,
A journey kissed by starlit gleams.

In secret glades, where shadows blend,
Together we write, where dreams transcend.
In echoes of the night, we play,
Crafting love in celestial sway.

Celestial Whispers

Stars align in night's embrace,
Whispers soft of time and space.
Moonlight dances on the sea,
Carrying dreams, wild and free.

Comets trace their fleeting paths,
In the silence, nature laughs.
Echoes of a cosmic tune,
Singing softly to the moon.

Galaxies in velvet skies,
Twinkling like our secret sighs.
Celestial spirits intertwine,
Guiding hearts with light divine.

Waves of starlight fill the air,
A gentle hush that calms the care.
In the night, our souls ignite,
Lost in whispers of delight.

Night's Dreaming Lamp

In the dark, a lantern glows,
Casting light where shadows grow.
Thoughts like clouds begin to drift,
In the stillness, spirits lift.

Crickets sing their lullabies,
Underneath the painted skies.
Every flicker tells a tale,
Of brave hearts that will not fail.

Dreams take flight on gentle breeze,
Carried through the whispering trees.
Night's embrace, a tender friend,
Holding close until the end.

With each star, a wish is spun,
In the glow of evening's sun.
Night's dreaming lamp will always shine,
Guiding hearts through space and time.

Slumbering Constellations

In the heavens, stories sleep,
Stars will watch, while shadows creep.
Constellations hold their dreams,
Whispering soft celestial themes.

Orion guards the night so grand,
With his bow and steadfast stand.
Pleiades in silken glow,
Cradle wishes, sweet and slow.

Galaxies in silent flight,
Painting patterns, pure delight.
While the world beneath is still,
Stars awaken, hearts they fill.

In the dark, they softly sway,
Guiding lost souls on their way.
Slumbering constellations gleam,
Holding tight to every dream.

Dreams Adrift in Twilight

Twilight drapes the world in gold,
Where secrets of the night unfold.
In this hour, dreams softly sing,
To the tunes the night will bring.

Glimmers fade, yet hearts awake,
Chasing shadows, paths we make.
Every sigh, a whispered thought,
In the twilight, battles fought.

Stars arise as day departs,
Filling voids within our hearts.
Wishing upon a fleeting light,
Guided by the hope of night.

Dreams adrift, like feathered clouds,
Float through silence, soft and loud.
In this time, we find our way,
Navigating shadows that play.

Navigating the Milky Way

In the vastness we drift and sway,
Stars guiding our night and day.
With each spark, we trace our fate,
In silence, we contemplate.

Galaxies swirl in a dance so bright,
We chase shadows, seeking light.
Through cosmic winds, our spirits soar,
Beyond the sky, forevermore.

Past the comets, old and wise,
Reflecting dreams in distant skies.
We chart a course through space's stream,
Woven threads of every dream.

Here in the silence of the void,
We find the beauty we enjoyed.
Navigating with hearts ablaze,
Through the Milky Way's endless maze.

Whispers from the Cosmic Sea

From deep within the cosmic sea,
Whispers flow, wild and free.
Each gentle wave, a silent call,
Binding together one and all.

Stars like pearls on midnight's bed,
Telling tales of those long dead.
In lullabies of ancient light,
Dreams awaken in the night.

Echoes dance through timeless space,
Tracing our steps through empty grace.
In each whisper, secrets lie,
Of worlds unseen, of endless sky.

In cosmic currents, we unite,
In the dark, we find our sight.
Listen close, let worries cease,
In the whispers, find your peace.

Cosmic Symphony of the Night

Under the veil of starlit dreams,
The universe plays in gentle beams.
Notes cascade like falling dust,
A symphony in time we trust.

Every twinkle, a note to behold,
In the quiet, a story unfolds.
Galaxies sing in vibrant hues,
A melody of cosmic views.

The moon conducts the endless choir,
Each heartbeat fuels our wild desire.
Through cosmic waves, let us dance,
In this symphony of fleeting chance.

As night envelops, we take flight,
In harmony, we chase the light.
With every pulse, we touch the sky,
In this cosmic song, we fly high.

Dreaming in the Light of Midnight

In the cradle of the midnight glow,
Dreams awaken, secrets flow.
Underneath a blanket of night,
Whispers of fate take their flight.

Moonlit paths begin to weave,
A tapestry only we perceive.
With every star, our hopes ignite,
In the soft embrace of twilight.

Time stands still, the world asleep,
In starlit depths, our promises keep.
We journey forth with hearts so bold,
In the warmth of dreams we hold.

In the night's embrace we glide,
With each pulse, we turn the tide.
Dreaming sweetly, we'll find our way,
In the light that wraps the day.

The Dreams of Astral Wave

A whisper drifts through starlit skies,
Where dreams take shape in cosmic sighs.
Each wave a thought, a wish, a plea,
In the ocean vast, we long to be.

Glowing orbs of night's embrace,
Guide weary souls to a sacred place.
With colors bright, they paint the night,
In a dance of fate, we find our light.

Rippling echoes of hope unwind,
As stardust falls, our hearts align.
In silence deep, our spirits soar,
On astral waves, forevermore.

To dream beneath the endless dome,
In waves of light, we find our home.
With every pulse, a journey starts,
In dreams of waves, we heal our hearts.

Nightfall's Cosmic Caress

In velvet hues, the night unfolds,
A cosmic tale through stars retold.
With tender light, the heavens smile,
And wrap the world in dreams awhile.

The moon whispers secrets of the past,
While comets trail, their beauty vast.
In twilight's grasp, we lose our fears,
And find solace in the cosmos' tears.

Galaxies swirl in a gentle spin,
As night's embrace invites us in.
The universe hums a lullaby,
Beneath the canvas of the sky.

In cosmic arms, we drift and sway,
Lost in the magic of night's ballet.
With every star that graces sight,
We find our peace in endless night.

A Dance Among Celestial Chords

In the hall of stars, a chorus sings,
Where harmony with eternity clings.
Notes of wonder flow between,
In the dance of light, we are seen.

Every twirl ignites the dark,
With rhythms that leave a radiant mark.
In synchronicity, we align,
As cosmic strings in patterns twine.

Galactic whispers weave a tune,
Under the watch of a silver moon.
With fervent hearts, we sway and glide,
Through the melody of the night, we ride.

To dance among the stars we crave,
In cosmic chords, our spirits wave.
In unity, our souls are free,
In this celestial symphony.

The Luminescent Path of Dreams

Beneath the stars, a path aglow,
Where dreams are born and spirits flow.
Each step we take in shimmering light,
Guides us through the veil of night.

With flickering hopes and gentle sighs,
We walk the bridge where wishes rise.
In the luminous haze, we find our way,
Through whispers of night and break of day.

A tapestry of dreams awaits,
Where every heartbeat resonates.
In hues of gold and silver streams,
We follow the path, the light of dreams.

As dawn approaches, shadows part,
With every step, we make a start.
In the glow of night, our souls agleam,
We journey forth on the path of dreams.

The Dancer in the Night Sky

In the velvet cloak of night,
Stars twirl with ethereal grace,
Each flicker a step in their dance,
Whispering secrets of space.

Moonlight spills like silver wine,
Gathering dreams on darkened ground,
A cosmic waltz in perfect time,
Where silence holds the sweetest sound.

Through the chill of midnight air,
Their movements paint the heavens wide,
A balletic ballet rare,
The universe, their stage and guide.

As dawn creeps in with gentle hues,
The dancers bow and say goodbye,
Yet in the moments of the blues,
They linger still in the night sky.

Cosmic Vistas of the Sleeping Mind

In slumber's arms, where dreams take flight,
Galaxies swirl in thoughts unknown,
A canvas brushed with starlit light,
Where cosmic wonders ever shone.

Nebulae bloom in the mind's retreat,
Each color whispers tales untold,
In the depths, where silence meets,
Imagination's wonders unfold.

Thoughts drift like comets through dark space,
Tracing paths of forgotten lore,
In this realm, we find our place,
Exploring what our souls adore.

When morning breaks, the visions fade,
Yet pieces of the night remain,
In waking hours, the dreams cascades,
A cosmic bond that can't be tamed.

Embracing the Always-Coming Night

As dusk unfurls its gentle hand,
The horizon sinks in shades of gray,
We gather 'round in silence planned,
   Embracing night, the end of day.

Stars emerge from their hidden beds,
   Painting shadows on the ground,
With distant whispers, softly spread,
In twilight's calm, their beauty found.

Through whispered winds, the darkness gleams,
   A soft cocoon of hidden grace,
   Awakening our wildest dreams,
In the night's arms, we find our place.

Though day retreats, the heart ignites,
   With every star a wish to fill,
We dance in time, embracing sights,
   In the quiet, we find our will.

Alight in the Galaxy's Hold

In the cradle of night's embrace,
Galaxies twinkle, dreams alight,
Each pulse a heart in endless space,
We collide with magic in our sight.

Through starlit paths and comet tails,
We journey forth without a fear,
In cosmic tides, our spirit sails,
Cradled close, the universe near.

With every breath, we feel the pull,
Of distant worlds and radiant beams,
In this vast realm, both bright and dull,
We navigate our woven dreams.

So take my hand, together we'll go,
Through the wonders that the night bestows,
In the galaxy's hold, we'll ebb and flow,
As starlight dances, endlessly glows.

Where Dreams Meet Stellar Waves

In a sea of shimmering light,
Dreams ride high on cosmic tides.
Whispers of stars guide the flight,
As the heart of the universe abides.

Gentle currents pull me near,
Softly cradled in night's embrace.
Each wave a tale, so crystal clear,
In this vast, enchanting space.

Echoes of ancient songs align,
Painting the sky in hues so bright.
Here, where galaxies intertwine,
The soul dances with sheer delight.

With every wish cast on the breeze,
I sail on dreams, forever free.
Amongst the stars, my spirit flees,
Where love and wonder come to be.

Dreaming Under Celestial Canopies

Beneath the vast and twinkling quilt,
I drift in realms of endless night.
Stardust weaves where dreams are built,
In a dance of ethereal light.

Clouds like feathers float above,
Whispers of hope softly sway.
In this place, I feel your love,
Guiding me through shadows' play.

Melodies of time echo clear,
Each note a spark in the still air.
With every breath, I draw you near,
Carried by twilight's serene glare.

Wrapped in the warmth of moonlit beams,
I wander through the endless night.
Awash in a sea of silver dreams,
Together, we take flight.

Nocturnal Whispers in the Moonlight

In the hush of night, secrets sigh,
Whispers dance in shadows tall.
Beneath the moon's watchful eye,
   Nature's lullaby softly calls.

Crickets chirp a soothing tune,
As fireflies twinkle in delight.
In this magic of the moon,
Every heartbeat feels just right.

Dreams unfurl like petals wide,
   Beneath a tapestry of stars.
In the quiet, hearts confide,
   Stories woven from afar.

With every breath, the night unfolds,
A symphony of love and light.
In the darkness, a warmth enfolds,
Guiding souls through endless night.

Slumbering Beneath a Cosmic Veil

As the universe draws its cloak,
I sink into a dreamlike haze.
Stars above softly provoke,
Inviting me to cosmic ways.

With every blink, worlds collide,
Galaxies swirl in gravity's waltz.
In this wonder, I confide,
Finding magic in the faults.

Nebulas paint the heavens bright,
A palette of colors so rare.
I drift in this celestial flight,
Weightless, free from worldly care.

Awake or asleep, who can tell?
In this realm where dreams attain,
I am cherished, I am well,
Dancing softly in the cosmic rain.

Elysium in the Realm of Dreams

In whispers soft the night unfolds,
A tapestry of starlit gold.
The moonlight bathes the world in grace,
As slumber's kiss we gently trace.

Fields of bliss, where spirits roam,
In every heart, a hidden home.
With laughter light and shadows long,
We weave the threads of an endless song.

Clouds of mist with secrets blur,
In this realm, my thoughts confer.
Each moment sings a different tune,
As dreams entwine beneath the moon.

Elysium calls with gentle sighs,
In the stardust, our spirit flies.
A harbor sweet where hopes ignite,
In this magic, we find our light.

Celestial Cradles and Cosmic Caresses

Beneath the stars, my spirit soars,
In cradles soft, where wonder pours.
A cosmic dance, the galaxies spin,
As gentle breezes pull me in.

The universe sings a lullaby,
In every heartbeat, a sigh.
Celestial tides that ebb and flow,
In whispers sweet, we come to know.

Galaxies twirl in velvet nights,
With every touch, our heart ignites.
A cosmic dance, so sweet, we share,
In cosmic caresses, love laid bare.

Stars align in tender light,
As dreams awaken in the night.
In celestial arms, we softly rest,
In this embrace, we are truly blessed.

A Dance of Light Beneath Closed Eyes

In quiet realms, where visions gleam,
A dance of light, a waking dream.
With every breath, the colors sway,
In rhythmic pulses, night meets day.

Beneath closed eyes, a world unfolds,
With stories written, yet untold.
The shadows move, a ballet grand,
In whispered breezes, hand in hand.

Light cascades in vibrant streams,
Awakening the heart's deep dreams.
A shimmered path, where hopes align,
In this embrace, our souls refine.

Each fleeting moment, a radiant spark,
In timeless dance, we leave our mark.
With eyes closed tight, we freely fly,
In the dance of light, we learn to sigh.

Painting the Sky on My Eyelids

With every blink, I see the skies,
Painted dreams in my closed eyes.
Strokes of pink, and shades of blue,
A masterpiece that feels so true.

Clouds of wonder float and play,
In vivid hues, they waltz away.
A canvas vast, where visions soar,
In breathless silence, I adore.

The sun dips low, a golden hue,
As twilight whispers, soft and new.
In this quiet, colors blend,
On my eyelids, dreams descend.

Stars emerge with slightest grin,
A gallery that draws me in.
Through painted skies, my heart's delight,
In every moment, a spark of light.

Dreamscapes in the Celestial Tapestry

In twilight's gentle glow we drift,
Where stars like whispers softly lift.
The dreams are woven, gold and bright,
In patterns stitched of silk and light.

Beneath the canvas vast and deep,
We gather secrets that we keep.
From galaxies, the tales unfold,
Of journeys sought and wonders told.

A tapestry of night and day,
In moonlit paths, we find our way.
With every thread, a story spun,
In dreamscapes where the starlight runs.

The universe in silence sighs,
As shadows dance and echoes rise.
Through every hue and cosmic line,
Our hearts entwined, forever shine.

The Galaxy's Caress

In starry arms, we find our peace,
Each twinkling light, a sweet release.
Galaxies swirl in cosmic tune,
Beneath the watchful, silver moon.

Embraced by night with velvet grace,
We wander deep through time and space.
The universe, a soft embrace,
In its vastness, we find our place.

Nebulae bloom like flowers bright,
A symphony of pure delight.
With every breath, the cosmos hums,
In every heart, a heartbeat drums.

With every gaze, we feel it near,
The galaxy whispers, calm and clear.
In cosmic bliss, our spirits soar,
In the galaxy's arms forevermore.

Dreaming of Celestial Shores

On shores of stars, we walk tonight,
With waves of dreams in celestial light.
The cosmos stretches, vast and wide,
With secrets held by the ocean's tide.

Each grain of stardust whispers low,
Of distant worlds, where wonders grow.
In twilight's calm, we take our stand,
With galaxies held in our hand.

The breeze of night sings soft and clear,
As constellations draw us near.
In every wave, a tale retold,
Of ancient myths and futures bold.

As dawn breaks through the velvet sky,
We chase the stars, we dare to fly.
On celestial shores where dreams align,
We find our home in love divine.

The Velvet Night's Embrace

In velvet night, our dreams take flight,
Suspended in the soft starlight.
With shadows deep and secrets spun,
The universe whispers, we are one.

Beneath a quilt of endless hue,
The moon's bright gaze feels fresh and new.
In cosmic lullabies, we sway,
As time slips softly, fades away.

The stars, they beckon us to dare,
To dance amongst the midnight air.
With every heartbeat, magic flows,
In night's embrace, the wonder grows.

As dawn approaches, dreams recede,
But in our hearts, they plant a seed.
In velvet night, where souls connect,
The universe loves and we reflect.

Celestial Navigation in the World of Sleep

In the quiet night sky, dreams take flight,
Stars whisper secrets in soft twilight.
Guided by the moon's gentle glow,
Paths of slumber begin to flow.

Waves of slumber, a soothing tide,
Through cosmic currents, we gently glide.
Lost in a dance of shadows and light,
Navigating realms where spirits ignite.

Celestial maps in the mind unfold,
Stories of ancients, silently told.
Each twinkling star, a beacon so bright,
Leading us home through the velvet night.

When dawn breaks, dreams softly fade,
Yet in our hearts, the night's serenade.
A journey through stars, now memory's keep,
Celestial navigation in the world of sleep.

A Universe Wrapped in Midnight

In the cradle of night, where shadows lie,
The universe dances, with a sigh.
Wrap me in darkness, a soft embrace,
In this realm of quiet, I find my space.

Galaxies spin in a slow waltz,
Whispers of cosmos, free of faults.
Stars bloom like flowers, each one a dream,
In the midnight canvas, a silver seam.

Nebulas swirl like colors in ink,
Painting the void that makes my heart sink.
Time suspends in the cool, crisp air,
As I wander in realms beyond compare.

Here in the dark, my spirit takes flight,
Embracing the wonders of endless night.
A universe wrapped in midnight's grace,
In stars, I find my rightful place.

Constellations of the Mind's Eye

In the theater of thought, stars align,
Filling the canvas with dreams divine.
Constellations swirl in a cosmic ballet,
Guiding my heart as I drift away.

Thoughts intertwine like galaxies spun,
Each one a story, a race well run.
Through nebulous clouds of vibrant hue,
In the mind's eye, the universe grew.

With each flicker of light, a truth revealed,
Hidden within, emotions concealed.
Mapping the joy, the pain that I see,
Constellations whisper, setting me free.

In this vast expanse of my inner space,
I find my purpose, my rightful place.
A journey through stars, bold and wise,
Exploring the constellations of the mind's eye.

The Silence of Distant Lights

In the dark, a quiet hush reigns,
Echoes of silence fill the plains.
Stars shimmer softly, a gentle might,
In the stillness of distant lights.

Each twinkle a story, a cosmic song,
Whispers from worlds where we belong.
Time stretches thin as I stare in awe,
Suspended in wonder at the vast, pure law.

Galactic mysteries weave through the night,
Veils of existence cloaked in soft light.
A tapestry woven with threads of peace,
The silence of stars grants our hearts release.

Though millions of miles may keep us apart,
In the stillness, we feel the same heart.
Under this canopy, our hopes take flight,
Embracing the silence of distant lights.

Journeying Through Cosmic Silhouettes

In endless night, we drift along,
Stars whisper tales, gentle and strong.
Nebulae swirl with colors bright,
Guiding our hearts like bees to light.

With every step, we leave a trace,
Merging dreams with time and space.
The cosmos breathes, a rhythmic sigh,
Awakening wonders that never die.

Galaxies wink in cosmic dance,
Through velvet skies, we take our chance.
Each comet's flame, a fleeting spark,
Illuminating paths in the dark.

Together we'll chase the outer gleam,
In a universe vast, we dare to dream.
With every heartbeat, stars align,
In cosmic silhouettes, your hand in mine.

The Sound of Celestial Laughter

Echoes of joy float through the night,
Stars chuckle softly, a pure delight.
Milky Way sings a lullaby sweet,
As cosmic beings sway to the beat.

A symphony born from the sky's embrace,
Soft whispers of warmth in the endless space.
Galactic giggles twinkle and gleam,
Filling the void with laughter's dream.

In every twirl, a star's bright cheer,
We listen closely, the music near.
Galaxies spin, as if in jest,
Inviting us to join the fest.

The universe plays a cosmic tune,
Under the watch of the glowing moon.
In this stillness, hearts leap and soar,
For in celestial laughter, we find the core.

The Night Paints Diagrams Beneath My Eyelids

When darkness falls, a canvas gleams,
Whispering secrets through silent dreams.
Constellations sketch with gentle hands,
Blueprints of hopes from distant lands.

Beneath closed lids, wonders arise,
Mapping the flight of starry skies.
Each twinkling light spins stories old,
Of daring hearts and journeys bold.

Colors swirl in the midnight hue,
Imagined tales both bright and blue.
The night reveals what daylight hides,
In cosmic diagrams where love abides.

Awake through dreams, we wander free,
On paths painted by a galaxy.
The night unfolds mysteries untold,
Creating magic in whispers bold.

Reveries Danced Amongst Galaxies

Amidst the stars, our spirits soar,
In reverie's arms, we explore.
Galactic whispers rise and fade,
A dance of dreams, serenely laid.

Twilight's caress wraps us in light,
Where dreams and cosmos unite in flight.
With every heartbeat, our souls ignite,
Within this waltz of the endless night.

Twirling through space, we find our place,
In the grand ballet of time and grace.
Nebulas swirl in colors rare,
Painting our journey in cosmic air.

As stardust settles, we breathe deep,
Harvesting treasures the heavens keep.
In reveries of galaxies, we blend,
A timeless dance that knows no end.

Crystal Dreams of the Cosmos

In twilight's hush, the stars ignite,
Whispers soft, a cosmic flight.
Jewels bright in velvet skies,
Each a dream that never dies.

Galaxies twirl, a dance divine,
Fragments of time in endless line.
Mirrors of hope, they shimmer and gleam,
Carrying wishes in each beam.

Comets race with tails of light,
Carving paths through the velvet night.
In the quiet, hearts take wing,
Echoes of joy that starlight brings.

The universe cradles each sweet thought,
In its embrace, solace is brought.
Crystal dreams, we softly weave,
In the cosmos, we believe.

Celestial Serenade

Underneath the moon's soft glow,
Celestial tunes begin to flow.
Stars pluck strings in harmony,
A symphony of galaxies.

Silver notes on gentle breeze,
Whirling softly through the trees.
Whispers flutter, secrets sung,
An age-old tale to which we're strung.

Timeless echoes brush the night,
As constellations join the flight.
Each twinkle a melodic sigh,
Floating dreams in the vast sky.

In the silence, we converge,
Lost in rhythm, hearts emerge.
Celestial serenades we hear,
Songs of wonder, pure and clear.

When Dreams Take Flight

In shadows deep, our hopes ignite,
Wings unfold in the soft twilight.
Beyond the clouds, the world expands,
As dreams take flight, guided by hands.

Whispers of joy, like feathers, soar,
Chasing sunsets, we long for more.
Horizons beckon with golden light,
When dreams take flight into the night.

Stars align, a path is drawn,
With every heartbeat, a new dawn.
Adventure calls, our spirits rise,
To chase the echoes of the skies.

Let fears dissolve like morning mist,
Embrace the thrill, the ardent twist.
When dreams take flight, we feel alive,
In the embrace of hope, we thrive.

A Sojourn Among the Celestial Bodies

Beneath the veil of night's embrace,
We wander through the vast expanse.
With every step, the cosmos speaks,
In silent awe, our spirit seeks.

Nebulas swirl in colors bright,
Painting wonder on the night.
Planets dance in lively play,
Guiding travelers on their way.

Galactic threads weave tales untold,
In the warmth of starlight, bold.
With every heartbeat, we explore,
A journey through the cosmic lore.

Amongst the wonders, dreams take form,
Under celestial skies, we're reborn.
A sojourn that fuels our souls,
In the universe, we find our roles.

Soaring Through the Milky Essence of Night

Under stars that softly gleam,
We drift through a silver dream.
Galaxies spin in gentle flow,
In the night's embrace, we glow.

Whispers of the cosmic air,
Calling us without a care.
Floating past the moonlit shores,
Lost in time, we seek for more.

Nebulas swirl in hues so bright,
Painting paths in the velvety night.
Each twinkle hides a silent tale,
As we watch the wonders sail.

Through the darkness, dreams ignite,
Soaring high, hearts taking flight.
In the vastness, we find our place,
In the Milky Essence's embrace.

A Journey Beyond the Lattice of Sleep

In whispers soft, the night unfolds,
As dreams begin, and time beholds.
A tapestry of stars is spun,
In shadows where the moonlight runs.

Each thread a tale, a secret keep,
A journey whispers through the deep.
Drifting gently, emotions sigh,
Beyond the lattice, we fly high.

With every heartbeat, realms unwind,
Waking worlds of the wandering mind.
In the stillness, visions bloom,
As clarity breaks through the gloom.

A journey vast, unknown, and bright,
Beyond the veil of silent night.
We seek the dreams that softly creep,
Into the spaces of our sleep.

Whirling in the Softness of Celestial Beams

In the glow of starlit streams,
We dance within celestial dreams.
With every swirl of cosmic light,
The heart takes wing, embracing flight.

Through the haze of twilight's veil,
We spin on paths where wonders sail.
Galactic winds caress the soul,
In this softness, we are whole.

Each heartbeat beats in cosmic time,
As we drift in rhythm, pure and sublime.
In the depths of this gentle sway,
We chase the dawn, we greet the day.

With laughter echoing through the space,
We twirl in the universe's embrace.
Whirling in love, in light, in beams,
Forever lost in joyful dreams.

Navigating the Seas of Cosmic Reverie

On cosmic waves, we set our sail,
Navigating stars like ships in a tale.
The universe whispers, guides us near,
To realms of wonder, far and clear.

With stardust maps in hand we roam,
Through vast expanses, we find our home.
Celestial oceans of shimmering light,
In boundless beauty, we unite.

Each ripple tells a story old,
Of brave explorers and dreams untold.
We voyage forth with hearts aglow,
In the seas of reverie, we flow.

With every wave, our spirits rise,
To touch the truth beyond the skies.
Navigating with love as our plea,
In this eternal cosmic sea.

Cosmic Journeys in Rest

Stars whisper low, secrets of the night,
Drifting through realms, where shadows take flight.
Dreams are the vessels, they glide and they soar,
In the vast, endless space, we find so much more.

Nebulas cradle, the lost and the found,
While galaxies spin, in a dance all around.
The cosmic embrace wraps us snug and tight,
Guiding our souls through the depths of the night.

In stillness we wander, through time and through dreams,
Where starlight ignites all our silent screams.
The universe hums, a soft lullaby,
As we float in the ether, beneath the vast sky.

So let go, dear traveler, of worry and dread,
For in cosmic journeys, there's peace to be fed.
Rest now on this voyage, let the stars be your guide,
In dreams of the cosmos, let your spirit abide.

Sleep's Galactic Tapestry

A woven expanse of night's soft embrace,
Patterns of stardust, in time and in space.
Threads of the cosmos gently intertwine,
Creating a quilt, so divine and so fine.

Each slumbering soul, a bright shooting star,
Drifting in silence, no matter how far.
In realms of the arcane, we find our way home,
Among the celestial, forever to roam.

Nebulae dream with colors alive,
As the night shall cradle, our spirits derive.
A tapestry grand, of dreams sewn with care,
In the quiet of night, our hearts find repair.

So let the vast cosmos cradle your head,
As night wraps her arms, and we welcome the bed.
Sleep's galactic whispers will guide you to light,
In the enchanting embrace of the infinite night.

Heavenly Lullabies

The moon sings softly, a lullaby clear,
Notes made of starlight, for every dear sphere.
Tender the echoes, each whispered refrain,
Cradling the world in a soothing domain.

Comets sweep past with a gentle caress,
Showering dreams in a cosmic press.
Each twinkling star holds a promise anew,
Cradled in slumber, the universe too.

In the silence of night, our worries take flight,
As stardust surrounds us, we drift without fright.
Heavenly songs flow like rivers of peace,
Binding the weary in comfort, in lease.

So close your eyes tight, let the night interlace,
With melodies woven in celestial grace.
For in this sweet moment, we're wrapped up in love,
Singing with angels, the stars up above.

Moonscape Musings

Upon the moonlight, reflections shall dance,
In tranquil musings, we find our romance.
Shadows weave stories under night's spell,
Inviting the heart in a silvery swell.

Milky Way whispers tales of the past,
While lunar soft beams cast a spell unsurpassed.
Each crater has wisdom, each path has a guide,
In the moonscape, secrets and wonders reside.

Gazing at beauty, we ponder and dream,
As our thoughts take flight on a soft, silver beam.
The world fades away in this mystical glow,
In the moon's gentle light, our dreams freely flow.

So linger a while, let your mind drift away,
In the hush of the night, where the shadows play.
Moonscape musings lead us to see,
The magic of night, forever we'll be.

Flickers of Night's Embrace

Stars whisper secrets, soft and light,
Moonlit shadows dance, taking flight.
The world sleeps deep, in peaceful sighs,
While dreams cascade, beneath dark skies.

Flickers of warmth in the chill of night,
Heartbeats in rhythm, a guiding light.
Through winding paths of slumber's grace,
Embraced by the night, a tranquil space.

In the stillness, magic unfurls,
Stories of wonder, in soft swirls.
Every flicker tells of fate and chance,
As the night cradles a mystic dance.

So let your thoughts drift, free as air,
In the flickers' glow, lose every care.
For the night is here, with a gentle trace,
A soothing balm in night's embrace.

The Interstellar Lullaby

Through cosmic paths where shadows roam,
Whispers of the stars invite us home.
Galaxies spin in an endless waltz,
Cradling dreams, where time halts.

A lullaby sung by celestial choirs,
Woven in light from distant fires.
Each note a spark, a timeless flight,
Echoing softly, the heart's delight.

Planets sway in the velvet deep,
Guardians of secrets that they keep.
Close your eyes, let the silence guide,
In this lullaby, let worries hide.

As comets race with tails aglow,
Feel the pulse of the cosmos flow.
Breathe in the magic, every sigh,
In the stillness of the interstellar sky.

In the Hush of Cosmic Dreams

In the hush where shadows play,
Whispers of stardust drift away.
Silken night drapes the slumbering ground,
In cosmic dreams, peace is found.

Nebulae dance in colors bright,
Cradled softly by the silk of night.
Every heartbeat syncs with the stars,
Guiding us gently through the bars.

Drifting on waves of endless skies,
We navigate through the night's lullabies.
In dreams we wander, wild and free,
In the hush of night, just you and me.

So let the cosmos weave its tale,
As time dissolves in the nightingale.
Together we'll soar, in this sweet scheme,
In the hush of our cosmic dream.

Infinity Wrapped in Velvet

In shadows deep, infinity glows,
Wrapped in velvet where the soft wind blows.
Endless echoes in the night,
Whispering secrets, hidden from sight.

Stars adorn the fabric of time,
Each a spark, a rhythmic rhyme.
Floating softly in eternal space,
Embraced by the unknown's grace.

Boundless and vast, horizons blend,
Where the journey of dreams transcends.
In velvet whispers, problems cease,
Finding refuge in starlit peace.

So lose yourself in this dark embrace,
In the infinity that time can't erase.
For within the night, we find our place,
Wrapped in velvet, our spirits trace.

Nebulous Visions Beneath Light's Embrace

In twilight's grasp, the shadows dance,
Whispers of night in a gentle trance.
Stars like pearls in velvet skies,
Painting dreams in wandering eyes.

Amidst the haze, our thoughts take flight,
Guided by hope, away from the night.
With every breath, a story unwinds,
Beneath the glow, our souls entwined.

Fleeting moments, a silken thread,
Caught in the web of words unsaid.
We drift together, lost in the glow,
A cosmos where only dreamers go.

Held by the light, our hearts in tune,
Swaying softly to a whispered tune.
In nebulous visions, we find our place,
Bound by the magic of time and space.

Ethereal Dreams and Midnight Skies

As shadows weave through the silent night,
A tapestry of stars holds tight.
Whispers of dreams float on the breeze,
Cradling wishes like autumn leaves.

In quiet corners where hopes reside,
Ethereal visions, our hearts collide.
Moonlit paths guide our weary feet,
To realms where the time feels sweet.

Beneath the veil of a midnight hue,
We share the secrets known by few.
A dance of souls, both young and old,
In dreams of magic, our stories told.

Awake or asleep, we venture far,
Chasing the glow of the evening star.
In the embrace of night, we find our way,
Living the dreams that refuse to fray.

Chasing Comets in Subconscious Spaces

Through the echoes of an endless night,
Comets streaking, a wondrous sight.
Charting courses through realms unknown,
In subconscious seas, we are not alone.

Every thought a spark, igniting the dark,
With trails of light, we leave our mark.
Wandering stardust, we drift and sway,
In the dance of time, we find our way.

Whispers of ages, both far and near,
Guide us gently, quelling our fear.
With every comet that passes by,
We capture dreams and learn to fly.

In the vastness where the wild things play,
We chase the wonder, come what may.
For in this space, alive and free,
Chasing comets, we dare to be.

Moons of Memory in the Depths of Rest

As night descends, the world transforms,
Wrapped in silence, the calm restores.
Moons of memory glow softly bright,
Guiding us gently through the night.

In peaceful corners, the heartbeats slow,
In restful realms where dreamers go.
Holding reflections like fragile glass,
We wander through time, let moments pass.

Each moon a story, each glow a sigh,
Echoes of laughter beneath the sky.
With shadows lingering, our fears allayed,
In the depths of rest, our dreams portrayed.

So let us drift where the memories play,
In the arms of night, we quietly stay.
In the luminous glow of past's embrace,
Moons of memory light our space.

Milton Keynes UK
Ingram Content Group UK Ltd.
UKHW052021251024
450245UK00012B/629